NOW YOU CAN READ....
ELIJAH

STORY RETOLD BY ARLENE ROURKE

ILLUSTRATED BY GWEN GREEN

Library of Congress Cataloging in Publication Data

Rourke, Arlene, 1944-
  Elijah.

  (Now you can read—Bible stories)
  Summary: A simple retelling of the Old Testament
story about the prophet Elijah and how he proved the
existence of God.
  1. Elijah, The Prophet—Juvenile literature.
2. Bible.   O.T.—Biography—Juvenile literature.
3. Bible stories, English—O.T. Kings.   [1. Elijah, the
Prophet.   2. Bible stories—O.T.]   I. Title.   II. Series.
BS580.E4R63   1986   222'.5309505   86-13061
ISBN 0-86625-320-3

Published by Rourke Publications, Inc., P.O. Box 3328, Vero
Beach, Florida 32964. Copyright © 1986 by Rourke Publica-
tions, Inc. All copyrights reserved. No part of this book may
be reproduced in any form without written permission from
the publisher. Printed in the United States of America.
  The Publishers acknowledge permission from Brimax
Books for the use of the name "Now You Can Read" and
"Large Type For First Readers" which identify Brimax Now
You Can Read series.

GROLIER ENTERPRISES CORP.

NOW YOU CAN READ....
ELIJAH

Many years ago, the king of Israel was a man named Ahab. The capital of Israel was a city called Samaria. Ahab lived in a great palace in Samaria.

Ahab had taken as his wife a woman named Jezebel. Jezebel was a proud and selfish woman. She was a Phoenician princess. Phoenicia was a country near Israel. The Phoenicians did not believe in the God of the Israelis. They believed in a god named Baal.

After Ahab married Jezebel he
turned away from his God and
began to worship Baal. He even had
a temple built in Baal's honor. He
encouraged his people to worship
Baal also. Jezebel brought many
prophets of Baal to Israel to take
care of the temple.

To be sure that Baal would be the most important god in Israel, Jezebel ordered her soldiers to kill all the prophets of the God of Israel.

God looked upon the wickedness of Ahab and Jezebel and He was very unhappy.

Now, living in Samaria at that time was a holy man named Elijah. He was one of the great prophets of the God of Israel.

One day, God appeared to Elijah and said to him: "Go to Ahab. Tell him that I know that he has turned against me. Tell him to repent his wicked ways. As a sign of my anger the rain will not fall for many days."

Elijah went to Ahab and told him what God had said. Ahab's faith in the true God was weak. Alas, he did not repent!

As God promised, the rain did not fall. The crops died. There was famine. Still, Ahab did not repent. Again, God appeared to Elijah. He told Elijah what he must do. Elijah began right away.

Elijah sought out another holy man. His name was Obadiah. Obadiah had hidden many of the prophets of Israel so that they would not be killed by Jezebel's soldiers. He had saved many lives. "You must go to Ahab and tell him I will meet him in the wilderness," Elijah said to Obadiah.

At first, Obadiah was afraid. He knew that Jezebel hated him and might try to kill him. But, his faith was strong. He hugged Elijah and promised that he would do as Elijah asked.

Ahab heard Obadiah's words and went to see Elijah.
"Why do you trouble Israel so, Elijah?" Ahab asked.

"It is not I who troubles Israel but you," Elijah answered. "God has seen all your wicked deeds. You have been given power and wealth and you have misused them. You have been greedy. You have treated your people unjustly. You have set false gods before the true God."

Ahab stood very still. He said nothing.

"God has decreed that Baal's power should be tested," Elijah went on. "You will order the prophets of Baal and the people of Israel to meet with me on Mount Carmel."

Ahab sent out word and the people of Israel gathered on Mount Carmel.

Also present were 450 prophets of Baal. They were dressed in rich robes with gold and jewels.

Elijah wore a simple robe and sandals.

He stood before the people and spoke: "Some of you have turned away from your God. You have worshipped the false god Baal. Your faith is weak. Before this day is over, you will see the power of the true God."

With that, Elijah ordered stones, wood and meat to be brought to the spot. "The prophets of Baal and I will each build an altar. They will build theirs to Baal. I will build mine to God. We will prepare a sacrifice but we will not light the fire. We will each call upon our God to light the fire."

The prophets of Baal began first. They laid the stones to make an altar and put wood on top of the stones. Over that, they placed the meat. Then, they stood back and prayed to Baal to accept their sacrifice by lighting the fire.

Everyone waited. Nothing happened.

Again, they called on Baal. Nothing. They shouted and begged. Nothing. Hours passed. Still no fire. The people were amazed.

It was late in the day and Elijah began to build his altar. First, he took twelve stones and laid them together. They stood for the twelve tribes of Israel.

Atop that, he put the wood and the meat. Around the altar he dug a trench. He ordered that twelve barrels of water be poured over the sacrifice.

Elijah raised his face to heaven and spoke: "Hear me so the people will know that you are the true God. Turn their hearts back again."

With that, the fire of God fell to the earth and the sacrifice burned brightly. The people dropped to their knees to worship God. Rain finally fell on the parched land.

When Ahab received word of this
great deed, he still refused to
repent. His faith in God was not as
strong as Elijah's or Obadiah's.
Sadly, there was no salvation for
Ahab.

All these appear in the pages of the story. Can you find them?

Jezebel

Elijah

Prophets of Baal

A soldier
of Jezebel

Ahab

Obadiah

Now tell the story in your own
words.